★ CELEBRITY ACTIVISTS ★

ENVIRONMENTAL CAUSES

GARY CHANDLER AND
KEVIN GRAHAM

Twenty-First Century Books

A Division of Henry Holt and Company

New York

Twenty-First Century Books
A Division of Henry Holt and Company, Inc.
115 West 18th Street
New York, New York 10011

Henry Holt® and colophon are registered trademarks of Henry Holt and
Company, Inc.
Publishers since 1866

Published in Canada by Fitzhenry & Whiteside Ltd.
195 Allstate Parkway, Markham, Ontario L3R 4T8

Printed in the United States of America on acid free paper. ∞

Created and produced in association with Blackbirch Graphics, Inc.

Library of Congress Cataloging-in-Publication Data

Chandler, Gary
    Environmental causes / Gary Chandler and Kevin Graham.
        p. cm.(Celebrity activists)
    Includes bibliographical references and index
    ISBN 0-8050-5232-1
    1. EnvironmentalismUnited States. 2. CelebritiesUnited
StatesCharities. 3. EnvironmentalistsUnited StatesCharities.
    I. Graham, Kevin, 1959   . II. Title. III. Series.
GE197.C36   1997
363.7–0574dc21
                                                                      9722266
                                                                          CIP

CONTENTS

INTRODUCTION

One of our finest American traditions is philanthropy—giving of ourselves, by either donating time or money, to those who need us. Helping the less fortunate is part of our heritage and is a quality that we can be proud of.

For many people who are very well known to the public, this sense of responsibility toward others is especially strong. Successful athletes, actors, musicians, business leaders, and others often accept their positions in the spotlight as role models, and they look for opportunities to give something back to their communities. These celebrities play important roles in helping charitable groups educate the public and raise money for a variety of causes. When a favorite baseball player or movie star asks people for their help in benefiting a cause, chances are good that

people are going to listen to the message and want
to show their support.

There are thousands of nonprofit organizations in the United
States that are working to improve our quality of life—whether
it is by ending hunger and child abuse, protecting the environment, increasing literacy and educational opportunities, or
helping to provide treatments and find cures for diseases.

In 1989, I established the Celebrity Outreach Foundation to
help charitable groups enlist the help of celebrities who support
their causes and are looking for opportunities to help. It was the
first organization of its kind in the country. To date, we have
matched more than 600 celebrities with 350 nonprofit organizations.

Before we could help anyone, however, we had to establish
our own credibility as a new foundation. Gregory Peck, Whoopi
Goldberg, Dan Aykroyd, Eddie Murphy, Alec Baldwin, Tony
Danza, and others stepped forward to support our efforts. A
Celebrity Advisory Committee was formed. The names of all
the committee members are featured in our promotion materials.
Without the committee's support, it would have been much more
difficult to establish our identity.

The celebrities featured in this book have all made major
commitments by contributing their time, money, and names to
help a variety of causes. (There are many others, but unfortu-
nately we do not have the space to include every philanthropic
celebrity.) Their efforts have made a significant difference in
the lives of many people.

Bob Oettinger
Celebrity Outreach Foundation

MUSICIANS
WORKING
FOR
CHANGE

For most musicians, writing songs and creating music involves much more than the simple task of coming up with lyrics and developing melodies. Their music often becomes an extension of their beliefs and desires.

Many musicians, as well as other types of performers, have chosen to use their influence as celebrities to have a positive impact on the future of humankind and the Earth. They have become involved in many different efforts to protect against threats to the natural world, including over-development of land and harmful pollution. They are leading projects to preserve land, educate children on environmental issues, and support a variety of environmental groups that are working to protect our environment.

Don Henley

In July 1845, Henry David Thoreau moved to Walden Woods in Massachusetts. He built a small cabin near the shores of Walden Pond where he lived for a few months. For the next two years, the great American author and conservationist wrote about his coexistence with nature. In the surrounding woods, he developed several theories of conservation that continue to guide today's environmental movement in this country and throughout the world. Thoreau's famous book, *Walden*, is considered one of America's greatest literary achievements.

More than 100 years later, Don Henley also explored nature—in the woods near his boyhood home in rural eastern Texas. Henley, who went on to become a famous rock-and-roll singer with the band The Eagles, loved to roam the woods with his dog.

"In the spring, I would don my raincoat and go walking in thunder-showers," Henley wrote in the book, *Heaven Is Under Our Feet*—a collection of environmental essays written by well-known Americans. "This little custom scared the living daylights out of my mother, who was certain I would be struck by lightning or swept away by the malignant elements."

Don Henley founded the Walden Woods Project to protect the area from commercial development.

During high school, Henley read Thoreau's *Walden*. And in college he learned more about Thoreau's reverence for nature and his philosophy on civil disobedience—a practice by which a person refuses to obey government laws or demands (usually through nonviolent protest) in order to influence government policy.

"Thoreau's writing struck me like a thunderbolt," Henley wrote. "Like all great literature, it articulated something that I knew intuitively, but could not quite bring into focus for myself."

Because of Thoreau's book, Walden Woods came to be known over the years as the birthplace of the American conservation movement. This was mainly due to the long-lasting impact of Thoreau's belief in the preservation of public land and the need to create a balance between humankind and the environment.

In 1989, however, Henley learned that Walden Woods was threatened by commercial development. Two projects were planned that would destroy historic and environmentally sensitive sites in the woods. One entailed a 147,000-square-foot office building just 700 yards from Thoreau's original cabin site. The other involved 140 condominium units only a half mile from Walden Pond.

Despite ongoing preservation efforts, half of Walden Woods still had no protection from commercial development and urban sprawl. This dilemma spurred Henley to found the Walden Woods Project in 1990. The nonprofit group is dedicated to preserving endangered land within the woods and has successfully saved large pieces of that land in recent years. It has accomplished this by raising money through memberships, benefit concerts, grants, and many other fund-raising activities.

In January 1991, with the help of the Trust for Public Land (TPL—a national land preservation organization), the Project purchased the 25 acres of land threatened by the condominium development for $3.5 million—well below what the property would have sold for to a commercial buyer. A year later, the Walden Woods Project purchased another 25-acre parcel of land right next to the lot bought the year before. Boiling Spring, which is a spot frequently mentioned in Thoreau's *Walden,* is located on this land.

The Walden Woods Project has protected nearly 100 acres of this historic site.

"The preservation of Walden Woods offers an invaluable opportunity for visitors from around the world to gain a better understanding of the origins of Thoreau's concepts of conservation.... More than half a million people visit Walden Pond and Walden Woods every year...," says Kathi Anderson, the Project's executive director.

Walden Pond is one of the many beautiful sites in Walden Woods.

In 1993, the Walden Woods Project reached an agreement with Boston Properties, the development company that owned the 18-acre office-park site near Thoreau's cabin. This agreement stopped the development of an office complex that would have been built on Brister's Hill, one of the primary locations where Thoreau studied the life stages of the forest, and one that he frequently mentioned in *Walden*.

To date, the Project has permanently protected nearly 100 acres of the historic woods. However, in spite of the Project's success, hundreds of acres in Walden Woods remain at risk. In addition, the Project has plans under way to make the area more accessible to the public in the form of a recreational and historic trail system.

"Walden Woods is the cradle of the American environmental movement and should be preserved for its intrinsic and symbolic value," Henley wrote in *Heaven Is Under Our Feet*. "We should make an effort to rekindle respect for the values that come from life lived in harmony with the land."

Paul Winter

Musician Paul Winter not only supports various ecological causes, he and the other musicians in his group, the Paul Winter Consort, incorporate the environment into the very music they create. Over the past 30 years, Winter has interwoven the musical traditions of many of the world's cultures with what he calls "the greater symphony of the earth." This symphony includes the sounds of wolves, whales, eagles, and several dozen other species of "wilderness musicians."

Since 1961, Winter has released more than 40 albums. In recent years, the Paul Winter Consort has been honored with two Grammy awards—both for best new age album of the year. In 1994, the Grammy was for the album, "Prayer for the Wild Things," and in 1993, "Spanish Angel." Winter had been nominated for five other Grammys earlier in his career.

Winter, who learned to play piano, saxophone, and clarinet as a child, first began playing in small bands with his schoolmates. He ventured out on his first professional tour at the age of 17. While attending Northwestern University and studying English composition, he formed the Paul Winter Sextet. The band won the 1961 Intercollegiate Jazz Festival and, soon after, signed a recording contract with Columbia Records.

The following year, the Sextet embarked on a lengthy and mind-opening 23-country tour of Latin America. It was sponsored by the U.S. State Department as a cultural exchange program. On this tour, the group learned some of the unusual rhythms of Brazil's bossa nova music. At the end of the tour, and at the invitation of First Lady Jacqueline Kennedy, the Sextet became the first jazz group to officially perform at the White House.

Winter formed the Paul Winter Consort in 1967, to further expand his exploration of the wide range of rhythms and melodies found in so many of the world's cultures. "I borrowed the name 'consort' from the ensembles of Shakespeare's time—the house bands of the Elizabethan Theater—which adventurously blended woodwinds, strings, and percussion," says Winter. "These were the same families of instruments I wanted to combine in my contemporary consort."

The following year, Winter first heard the songs of humpback whales and was fascinated with the idea of combining this form of nature's music with his own. At the same time, he also became interested in the plight of the wolf.

"The haunting blues-like celebration of a howling pack of wolves and the beautifully complex songs of the whales planted seeds of ideas that blossomed on a number of my later albums," Winter says. "We interwove the recorded sounds from the natural world with classical and ethnic traditions—the whole infused with the spontaneous spirit of jazz."

In 1977, Winter led a combined whale-watching and music-making expedition on Mexico's Baja Peninsula. This adventure cemented the ideas for "Common Ground," his first album that combined recorded sounds from nature with the Consort's distinctive music.

Paul Winter has incorporated the sounds of howling wolves into his music and has participated in educating schoolchildren about protecting the species.

Winter has performed and recorded his music in a wide variety of settings, such as Arizona's Grand Canyon, Israel's Negev Desert, New York City's Cathedral of St. John the Divine, and his barn-studio in Connecticut. He has awakened people to the plight of endangered species through the more than 2,000 concerts he has performed throughout Asia, Europe, and the Americas. About half of these concerts have benefited ecological organizations, such as the Predator Project, which protects endangered species; the Trust for Public Land; and the Whale and Dolphin Conservation Society.

Winter has also donated his time to make educational videos about the environment and frequently holds musical and ecological workshops to educate people on the importance of protecting the environment. To honor him for his musical contributions to the environment and the world's endangered species, the UN Environment Program presented Winter with one of its Global 500 Awards and its Award of Excellence in 1984. The album "Concert for the Earth," performed by the Paul Winter Consort in the UN's General Assembly Hall, helped officially observe World Environment Day that year and became the first jazz album ever recorded at the United Nations.

In a most unique honor years before, the Consort's album "Road" was taken to the Moon aboard *Apollo XV*. The mission's astronauts ended up naming two craters after the album's songs "Icarus" and "Ghost Beads."

"People get a sense of community from our music," Winter says. "A sense of the whole community of life, which is one of the best things we could do with our music. We hope we awaken a spirit of involvement in people for the preservation of wildlife and the natural environments of the Earth."

★ *Indigo Girls* ★

Since the beginning of their professional career in 1986, the Indigo Girls have released 7 albums, performed at more than 1,200 concerts, and received 5 Grammy nominations and 1 Grammy award. They also appeared in the major motion picture, *Boys on the Side,* and have sold more than 6 million albums in the United States.

Beginning in 1991, Emily Saliers and Amy Ray, who make up the folk-rock duo, turned their musical energies toward political activism. The group has worked to support the rights and protect the environment of Native American communities across the United States and Canada.

"We've always been political. We started out early in our career with environmental causes, doing a lot of Greenpeace benefits," said Ray, in an interview published in the December 1996 issue of *The Progressive* magazine. "Then in 1991, we took part in a show in New York City, called 'Ban the Dam Jam.' It was part of a wide effort to keep New England states from contracting with Hydro-Quebec, which was building the James Bay hydroelectric project mostly on Native lands."

Since 1991, the Indigo Girls have worked to benefit Native American environmental issues.

Through their dealings with many Native American activists at the "Ban the Dam Jam," the Indigo Girls decided to wholeheartedly support a campaign called Honor the Earth. This effort's mission is to create awareness and support for Native American environmental issues, and to develop needed financial and political resources for the survival of sustainable native, or indigenous, communities. There are more than 300 U.S. Indian reservations threatened by environmental hazards, and 77 sacred sites have been disturbed by development activities.

"Emily and I felt that the indigenous environmental movement was really important because its approach was more down our alley," Ray said. "It was very grass-roots and winning a lot of battles. We felt it was important and effective."

The Indigo Girls' first Honor the Earth tour in 1993 covered three cities—Minneapolis, Minnesota; Madison, Wisconsin; and Des Moines, Iowa—and raised nearly $70,000 for indigenous grass-roots organizations. This tour also sparked the interest of thousands of fans who sent post cards to U.S. Secretary of the

Interior Bruce Babbitt, calling for the cleanup of radioactive soil at the Point Hope Indian village in Alaska. Public pressure from the tour helped prompt the U.S. Environmental Protection Agency to conduct cleanup work at the site.

In 1995, the duo did another concert tour for the effort, this time conducting a 21-stop Honor the Earth benefit tour that raised close to $300,000 for the campaign. This tour included

The Indigo Girls (right) perform at an Honor the Earth benefit with the group Ulali (left) in September 1996.

five free concerts on Indian reservations in Minnesota, South Dakota, New Mexico, Arizona, and Alaska, and highlighted environmental issues faced on these reservations. Funds from the tour were distributed to 45 Native American groups working to defend their homelands from environmental threats and protect their sacred sites. In addition, more than 25,000 postcards were mailed to key decision makers in government, asking for action on environmental issues such as logging and hazardous waste dumping.

In 1996, the Indigo Girls produced a benefit album for the Honor the Earth campaign, titled "Honor," which includes songs by other famous musicians such as Bonnie Raitt, Soul Asylum, Rusted Root, Matthew Sweet, and Toad the Wet Sprocket. There were also songs by Native American artists. All together, 20 artists donated new music for the recording.

Faye Brown, the group's campaign coordinator, said that the album served as an organizing tool. It included information about some of the issues the campaign addresses and gave statistics about environmental destruction on indigenous lands. It also let people know how they could join the Honor the Earth campaign. Postcards similar to the ones used on the tour were included so people could voice their concerns regarding various indigenous environmental issues.

The Honor the Earth campaign is a joint project of the Seventh Generation Fund, a Native American grant foundation; the Indigenous Women's Network, a coalition of more than 400 Native American women activists and organizations; and the Indigenous Environmental Network, an effort aimed at organizing support for threatened Native American communities. All of the money raised by the campaign is distributed by the Seventh

Generation Fund's board, which is made up solely of indigenous members. The money supports more than 200 Native American groups in need of environmental protection. For example, the Lubicon Cree Indians in northern Alberta, Canada, are working to stop the largest clear-cut logging operation in North America. And the Western Shoshone Indians of Nevada are fighting to keep their sacred Yucca Mountain from becoming a U.S. dumping ground for high-level nuclear waste. Most of the groups supported by Honor the Earth are small and run by volunteers who work out of their homes with low annual budgets. Many operate without phones, fax machines, or computers.

"Our belief is that Native people have been standing [up] for the Earth for generations and generations, and most Native groups today are struggling to obtain needed resources," Brown says. "If we can get the critically needed political and financial resources to the Native groups engaged in these battles and build public consciousness, we believe many more of these battles will result in victories for the environment."

"Grass-roots Native organizations and communities represent an effective social movement doing important work," says Saliers. "They are fighting clear-cutting, coal mining, toxic dumping and incinerators in a heroic battle to protect future generations. But they are isolated and cash poor. Because of our experience, we have rededicated ourselves to environmental activism, focusing on the survival of Native peoples. As non-Indians, we cannot sit by silently and watch the continued destruction of Native communities. This is more than just another environmental cause. The basic issues of human rights, justice, and our own survival are ultimately at stake."

⭐ *Sting* ⭐

Sting is an internationally known rock star. He has also appeared in movies and starred in "Three Penny Opera" on Broadway.

According to Sting, the deforestation of the world's rainforests is as much of a threat to life on Earth as nuclear war. That's why he and his wife are working to defend the Amazon rainforests and the native people who live there.

In 1987, Sting and his wife Trudie Styler traveled to South America. There they met the leader of an indigenous tribe called the Kayapo Indians. This chief, Chief Raoni, told the couple about the plight of his people who live in the rainforest and took them to see the damage for themselves.

"We flew over land that looked like a desert—red dust, tree stumps and a few head of cattle grazing poorly on this land," Sting remembers. Chief Raoni told Sting that ten years earlier, the ravaged land they were looking at was all healthy rainforest.

Recalling the trip in a 1990 video called *Spaceship Earth*, Sting said, "When we crossed a point where the rainforest began again, where the destruction ended, I realized how beautiful this thing is—it's like a

Sting and his wife Trudie Styler stand backstage at the Rainforest Foundation benefit concert with RFF supporters Julia Roberts and Lyle Lovett.

cathedral of green, magical, enormous, expansive beauty. And then you compare it to the destruction in front of it—which is just devastated.... It really made me want to try to do something." What Sting did was join forces with his wife Trudie, Chief Raoni, and conservationist Franco Sciuto to form the Rainforest Foundation (RFF) in 1989. The mission of the foundation is to support the indigenous people living in rainforest regions in their efforts to protect their environment from being destroyed.

The causes of rainforest destruction are numerous, but all are due to human activity. Mining, logging, and cattle operations have taken a tremendous toll on the delicate rainforests of the world. Slash-and-burn farming has also caused a great deal of destruction. For example, in Brazil, the government has been giving rainforest land to unprepared city dwellers to motivate them to leave the overcrowded city of Rio de Janeiro. These families then move to the jungle and are forced to quickly clear their land in order to begin raising crops and livestock. After a year or two, the fragile soil is exhausted of nutrients and will no longer sustain crops or cattle. These families must then move on and repeat this land-use mistake in order to survive. Over the years, thousands of families have cleared millions of acres of rainforest in this way.

Lyle Lovett performs at the 1997 Annual Rainforest Foundation benefit concert.

The largest rainforest in the world is in Brazil, and the second-largest is in Indonesia. Rainforests are also in tropical areas around the world, including other parts of South America, Central America, Southeast Asia, and parts of central Africa. Rainforests contain more than one third of the plant and animal species found on Earth—this does not include the thousands of species of plants scientists believe exist there but are yet undiscovered, and never will be at the current pace of destruction!

In South America, the Rainforest Foundation works with the people of the rainforest to teach them how to obtain the natural resources they need without harming the environment, violating their culture, or compromising their future. The foundation also helps these people protect and shape their individual rights under the government. The RFF increases awareness for the need to protect the rainforest and inspires broad participation in this effort.

Under the direction of Sciuto, RFF plans to expand its scope to encompass rainforests all around the world. The group is already working in Guyana to help the native people defend themselves against the threat that mining poses to the rainforest there.

With Sting's help, the organization has raised more than $6 million to date, allowing the RFF to protect an area in the Brazilian Amazon roughly the size of Switzerland. This area is home to the Menkragnoti Kayapo people. The foundation also helped the Panara Indians return to their ancestral territory, from which they were forcibly removed in 1975 by the Brazilian government in order to make room for a new highway construction project. The group also works to improve communication and education among the Indians.

To fund its activities, the RFF relies heavily on an annual Rainforest Foundation benefit concert at New York City's

Carnegie Hall. Sting gathers the talent and his wife Trudie is responsible for organizing the all-star line-up. In fact, the 1995 concert was described as the best concert of the year by the *New York Post*. It made more than $1.4 million for the foundation and featured Bon Jovi, Bruce Springsteen, Elton John, Billy Joel, Paul Simon, James Taylor, and, of course, Sting. The performers donate their time, and all proceeds benefit RFF's conservation projects.

Sting also uses his celebrity influence to solicit large donations within the entertainment industry for RFF. He has brought Chief Raoni on stage during concerts to promote understanding about the rainforest and was the first recording artist to insist that his CDs be released with minimal packaging.

Sting spoke out about his feelings regarding the plight of the rainforest and the efforts of RFF. "If the rainforests die, then my country is in danger, too. The people of Europe and North America are in as much trouble as the Kayapo and the other people of the Amazon. This is about the air we breathe, the food we eat, the water we drink.... It's like burning the kitchen down one day and expecting to eat the next.... It doesn't matter if you are a rock singer, taxi driver, a housewife, or a bank manager, we all have the same basic needs."

Celebrity involvement can help heighten people's awareness of the many environmental problems that exist. It can also help to enlist more support in finding solutions to those problems, and implementing them. When famous people become connected to an issue, the media usually covers the story. This publicity can draw added attention to a cause, increasing the number of people who understand it. When enough people become involved and call for action, change is much more likely to occur.

ACTORS
GET
INVOLVED

★ Robert Redford ★

Movie actor and director Robert Redford grew up in southern California in the 1940s and 1950s and witnessed massive development in that region year after year. When the population of Los Angeles exploded, he saw clean air and water turn a dingy brown.

"Our greatest asset—our natural environment—which had been taken for granted, suddenly evaporated like water from a desert," Redford says in a commentary that appeared in *Time* magazine. "People were spilling into the city, swarms by the day. And I watched as the city began to choke on the air of unchecked development. Freeways and shopping malls began to wipe out neighborhoods and fruit groves. Consumption was all that mattered. And it all seemed right then. It was symbolic of our war [World War II] victory. We were eager to return our energy back home. It was a time when the word 'development' was new and positive. A sign of health, freedom and progress."

But the subtle consequences of this rapid development began to build in the form of smog and polluted streams and coastlines, making Redford appreciate the scenic wilderness more than ever before. As a teen, he spent as much time as possible wandering through Yosemite National Park. He learned to climb there and even worked at the park.

Since the 1970s, Robert Redford has worked tirelessly to help preserve and restore America's natural beauty.

Then a baseball scholarship took him to the mountains of Colorado. After two years, he left the Rocky Mountains to pursue painting, followed by acting. He eventually went to live in the pristine mountains of Utah, an area he had come to love during his long car trips between Boulder, Colorado, and Los Angeles while he was in college.

In 1961, Redford bought land, which included a small existing ski area near Provo, Utah, in order to save it from being further developed. Ironically, he soon realized that the only way he could afford to permanently preserve the area was through partial responsible development. On 75 acres of the property, he created the Sundance Resort and an arts community, which opened in 1969.

"I found myself, like preservationists everywhere, in the development game. The only way to protect nature is to manage it like a business—in fact, to make it a business and devote your life to it. And that was the last thing in the world I wanted to do. In some ways, it's been a nightmare," he says.

Redford's current efforts include work to revise the 1872 Mining Reform Act. The reforms stated in this act would ensure that mining companies would pay fair market value for land they want to mine and that environmental safeguards would be set up to protect that land. He's also involved in a struggle to prevent the opening of a radioactive waste dump in Ward Valley, California, just a few miles from the Colorado River. And he continues his work to help preserve and restore America's national parks.

In 1996, Redford worked with a coalition of groups to achieve a partial environmental victory when President Bill Clinton designated about 1.7 million acres in southern Utah as the Grand Staircase-Escalante National Monument—preserving it from development.

Redford had worked with the coalition to save 5.7 million acres of wilderness in Utah, an issue of debate in the state for decades. "Currently, 22 million acres of Bureau of Land Management land is held in trust in Utah. This land contains the world's most spectacular red rock country, and irreplaceable Native American ruins," Redford said in *USA Weekend.* "Protecting 5.7 million acres of this would still leave more than 16 million acres for economic development. It seems like enough to me, but Utah's politicians, along with powerful corporate special interests, crafted this so-called *wilderness bill* that protects only about 1.8 million acres. They say this is a balanced compromise. That is a misrepresentation—this is not a fair deal. I see the West con-tinually abused for short-term gain." The campaign to save an additional 4 million acres continues.

Although reckless development is one of Redford's many environmental concerns, his efforts have been quite diverse. In 1995, he lobbied Congress about the threat of weakening environmental protections in America. In 1993, he testified before the U.S. House of Representatives Natural Resources Committee about the contract to sell concessions at Yosemite National Park. He and others believed that the contract lacked appropriate environmental regulations.

Although Redford is best known for his conservation efforts in the American West, he knows that environmental problems such as air pollution have no borders. In 1989, he organized the Sundance Global Warming Summit, a meeting between leaders of the United States and the former Soviet Union to discuss global warming—and ways to curb it.

Redford spent nearly two years organizing the summit, co-sponsored by the Soviet Academy of Sciences. Representatives from government, industry, and the media attended the conference at his Sundance Resort in Utah.

In opening comments, Redford told the attendees, "I myself am very honored to be part of an effort to rechannel our imaginations and our talents to a more positive end....It's time to get this kind of information out of the hands of scientists—who are very valuable—and into public understanding and into government policy. And the only thing that will move politicians is when they get pressure from the public. And the public can't do it until they understand what the problem is."

At the conclusion of the summit, environmental experts wrote a letter to Presidents Bush and Gorbachev urging them to immediately support energy efficiency, limit greenhouse gas emissions, help save the rainforests, and promote citizen action.

"We can't wait for government, we can't wait for Congress, we can't wait for leadership—we have to just start acting. People themselves can do this," Redford says.

Redford has been leading by example for decades now. During the early 1970s, Redford joined with several environmental organizations to successfully oppose the plans for a coal-burning power plant in Utah. The land where the power plant would have been built is part of the 1.7 million acres now protected in the Grand Staircase-Escalante National Monument. Redford also stopped a four-lane highway from being built near his own property.

In addition, Redford has served on the boards of several environmental organizations, including the Natural Resources Defense Council, the Environmental Policy Center, the Wolf Fund, the Navajo Education and Scholarship Foundation, the Solar Lobby, the Smithsonian Institution, the Yosemite Institute, the Mountain Lion Foundation, and the Environmental Media Association.

In 1983, Redford founded the Institute for Resource Management (IRM). This unique effort brought environmentalists and industrialists together to resolve conflicts regarding the sustainable development of natural resources. Issues addressed included power sources, pollution, and many others. Although it provided an important platform for several years, IRM dissolved in 1989.

Redford's long-term environmental commitment has been recognized around the world. His many awards include the 1987 Global 500 Award from the United Nations Environment Program, the 1989 Audubon Medal Award, the 1993 Earth Day International Award, the 1994 Nature Conservancy Award, and the 1995 Condor Award from the California Indian Legal Services.

Ted Danson

Actor Ted Danson, who is best known for his role as Sam on the television show "Cheers," has been doing his part to remind society that healthy oceans are crucial to the survival of our environment.

Our oceans feed the world, cool our planet, regulate climate, and create nearly one half of the global oxygen supply. They also sustain biological diversity, provide us with leisure and recreation, and contribute significantly to the world's economy. In the United States alone, the coastal communities provide about 28 million jobs.

Despite the importance of our oceans, 3,500 U.S. beaches were closed temporarily in 1995 due to sewer contamination alone. Additional pollutants are causing even greater damage to the oceans.

"In just one generation—our generation—we are witness to the wholesale destruction of our oceans. Each day, billions of gallons of sewage, pesticides and industrial chemicals flow into the sea," Danson says. "Our commercially valuable fish stocks are in decline, severing a generation of fishers from a livelihood that has sustained them and fed us. Marine mammals are acquiring cancerous lesions from the accumulation of heavy and toxic metals. Quite simply, our arrogance is destroying us."

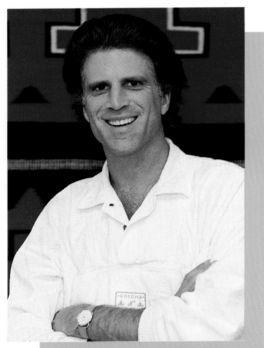

Ted Danson has been dedicated to saving our oceans for more than ten years and is president of the American Oceans Campaign.

Danson serves as president of the American Oceans Campaign (AOC). Established in 1987, the group works to educate both the public and policymakers about the need for establishing strong public policy to protect our marine resources. To accomplish its goals, AOC works with the government, public interest groups at the local and national levels, and private businesses.

Among the groups many efforts, AOC has diligently worked to strengthen the Clean Water Act by serving as co-chair of the Clean Water Network, an alliance of 800 citizen groups working to improve water quality. The AOC also has achieved a ban on the use of drift nets for fishing in American waters, and worked with the United Nations to reach an agreement to halt all Japanese and Korean drift net fishing in the high seas. Drift nets entangle and kill almost every living creature that comes in contact with them, including dolphins and whales.

In California, the AOC was responsible for permanently protecting the state from offshore oil drilling that was occurring in coastal waters. This has preserved the ecosystem of the coastline. It also developed the first-ever beach closure protocol for the county of Los Angeles. The protocol requires that public notice about health risks due to toxic or bacterial contamination be given to swimmers in the Santa Monica Bay. On the national level, the AOC has worked toward passage of the National Ocean Dumping Ban Act, which ended the dumping of inadequately treated sewage and sludge off U.S. coasts.

AOC has also produced several videos, television programs, and public service announcements regarding the need to keep our oceans and waterways healthy. In 1990, the group produced an award-winning "how-to" video titled *Help Save Planet Earth*. Danson helped recruit fellow celebrities Jamie Lee Curtis, Whoopi Goldberg, Sinbad, Sally Kellerman, Lloyd and Beau Bridges, John Ritter, and Milton Berle to assist and appear in the production. The group also co-produced *Danger At the Beach* with the National Audubon Society. This conservation film discussed the threats of pollution and aired on Turner Broadcasting stations and the Public Broadcasting System (PBS).

Estuary protection is now among AOC's top priorities. Estuaries are dynamic bodies of water along the coasts where freshwater flowing from streams meets and mixes with the salt-water of the ocean. The combination of freshwater and saltwater creates a unique environment in which aquatic plant and animal life thrives. Estuaries are often called by other names including bays, inlets, lagoons, sounds, and sloughs. About 45 percent of Americans live in estuarine areas, including Chesapeake Bay, Puget Sound, Long Island Sound, Tampa Bay, the Gulf of Maine, and San Francisco Bay.

For the last ten years, Ted Danson's hard work and commitment to the AOC has paid off. Although there is still much work to be done to regenerate and sustain the health of our oceans, this actor is dedicated to doing his share to protect the environment.

Meryl Streep ★

Thanks to actress Meryl Streep and her friend Wendy Gordon, families in America have greater access to pesticide-free food for their children.

When Streep and Gordon realized that their young children were being exposed to pesticide levels in food that exceeded what the government considered safe, they began demanding change. In 1989, they formed an organization called Mothers and Others for a Livable Planet. This group examines widespread environmental concerns, presents how certain concerns affect everyday life, and promotes sustainable alternatives in the marketplace. For example, Streep and Gordon began explaining how "safe" levels of pesticides had been set for adults, without considering that children are smaller, eat proportionately more fruits and vegetables than adults, and have growing bodies that may be more vulnerable to the effects of toxic pesticides.

Mothers and Others was created to protect children from foods with high levels of pesticides in them.

MOTHERS & OTHERS

For A Livable Planet

"Mothers and Others was founded out of concern for our children's health," says Streep. "We first organized around a kitchen table and began educating one another about what we can do to protect our children—and indeed ourselves and the planet—from high levels of pesticides in our food supply. Talk turned into action, and before long, we had persuaded our local supermarket in Connecticut to provide organic food."

Part of Streep's motivation for starting the organization came from doing research about apples. Her small children drank a lot of apple juice and she discovered that one pes-

Meryl Streep founded Mothers and Others with her friend Wendy Gordon in 1989.

ticide, called alar, couldn't be washed off the apples. Streep then found that there were more pesticides commonly lingering on fruits and vegetables. In addition, she learned that the toxic residues from these pesticides were even more dangerous for children because, pound for pound, they consume more fruits and vegetables than adults.

In 1989, Streep testified before Congress about the pesticide alar and its toxic residues on apples. Today, she feels the organization can claim much of the credit for the Food Quality Protection Act, which President Bill Clinton signed into law in 1996. The act outlaws many pesticides and increases the regulations on most others to help protect America's food and water supply. It also takes into account how much children weigh, not only adults, when determining allowable pesticide-residue levels on fruits and vegetables.

President Clinton said the act would give "...parents the peace of mind that comes from knowing that the fruits, the vegetables, the grains that parents put down in front of their children are safe." The act will establish health-based limits of all pesticide residues in food and prohibit risks being taken with pesticides for the sake of making profits. (It is more expensive to raise food without pesticides.) The act also requires the establishment of a new "right-to-know" network about pesticides in the food chain so that people are educated about the food they buy. Additionally, the new legislation will recommend guidelines for the National Academy of Sciences Committee on Pesticides in the Diets of Infants and Children.

Wendy Gordon (below) and Meryl Streep's organization played a big part in the passage of the Food Quality Protection Act.

In a different effort to cut down on the use of pesticides in the United States, Mothers and Others also promotes the growing of organic cotton. In 1994, U.S. farmers spent almost $800 million to dump nearly 50 million pounds of insecticides, herbicides, fungicides, growth regulators, and other pesticides on cotton crops alone. (And the numbers grew by about 30 percent in

1995.) In addition, almost 1 billion pounds of nitrogen fertilizer were used on U.S. cotton in 1994. Nitrogen fertilizer has been shown to cause blindness in farm workers, and it is not a substance that should end up in our rivers, streams, and groundwater.

Mothers and Others also works to promote organic alternatives to milk that comes from cattle injected with artificial growth hormones. In 1995, the U.S. Food and Drug Administration (FDA) approved the use of the bovine growth hormone (BGH). BGH is used to make dairy cattle produce more milk per day. Although economically desirable to the dairy farmer, the artificial growth stimulant has raised health concerns for many people. Mothers and Others began working to make more natural alternatives available. The group wants milk to be labeled so that consumers can distinguish between this milk and naturally produced milk.

Mothers and Others for a Livable Planet has more than 14,000 members and is quickly growing. Every three weeks the group publishes a six-page newsletter called *The Green Guide for Everyday Life,* and there are plans to start regional chapters around the country to help local leaders have a greater impact. Their toll-free number is (888) ECO-INFO, and they are on the internet at mothers@igc.apc.org. Thanks to organizations like Mothers and Others, the organic food industry in the United States has quadrupled in size since 1989, reaching annual sales of more than $2 billion.

In addition to her ongoing commitment to Mothers and Others, Meryl Streep has been involved in many other environmental projects, including the production of a television and video series for PBS called "Race to Save the Planet." In this series, Streep hosts ten episodes that explore several critical issues, including biological diversity, atmospheric disruption and destruction, rainforest depletion, and farming and politics.

★ Chevy Chase ★

Comedian Chevy Chase made a name for himself on the long-running comedy show "Saturday Night Live," and has continued to star in one hilarious movie after another. But Chase also has a serious side. He and his wife Jayni work with students around the world to improve environmental knowledge and stimulate positive actions.

In 1989, the couple realized that their three daughters were not learning about environmental issues at their California school, so they began accumulating information on their own to share with their children. Soon, they had assembled a library of information and began writing a book called *Project Eco-School: Blueprint for a Green Campus*. The book provides educational projects for students, and shows how schools and businesses can save energy and money with simple conservation measures. The book also led to a bigger venture for the Chases. *Project Eco-School* is now one of many educational products and services available through the Center for Environmental Education—a nonprofit organization founded by Chevy and Jayni Chase.

The mission of the organization is to ensure that every student in the United States receives an environmental education. The first step involved collecting vast amounts of information. The center now strives to distribute that information. Part of that distribution is a bi-annual newsletter, called *Grapevine*, that the center sends to more than 20,000 people. Among other things, it promotes networking and idea sharing as ways to spread environmental knowledge and concern.

Actor Chevy Chase has worked with his wife Jayni to promote environmental education for kids.

The Chases also developed a youth empowerment project, which includes partnerships between schools, students, and businesses. For example, high school students can adopt an elementary school and then prepare monthly educational presentations for the younger students for one school year. Another project allows students, with the help of school administrators, to conduct audits of environmental conditions at their school. They investigate things such as energy use and conservation, waste management and source reduction, food choices, supplies, and many other issues. The challenge is to find ways to minimize schools' negative environmental impact, which often saves participating schools sizable amounts of money in the process. The students also conduct the same audits at cooperating business locations in their community. The Center for Environmental Education is proud

Jayni Chase talks to students about environmental education.

of the environmental education it offers, but it also reminds parents and administrators of the health benefits.

"Children are far more vulnerable than adults to lead, pesticides, asbestos and toxic chemicals," Jayni Chase says. *"Blueprint for a Green Campus* puts reliable information at your fingertips, and hazardous substances are only one of several topics covered. Teachers have a tremendous responsibility to contribute to a healthy future for the planet. Environmental education should be a required part of every curriculum."

"We all have to do something to help heal the Earth," adds Chevy Chase. "Things are getting worse as we talk, and if we wait too long, we will seriously affect the Earth's ability to sustain our form of life."

Ed Begley, Jr.

Ed Begley, Jr., is best known for his role as Victor Ehrlich in the television series "St. Elsewhere," and his roles in movies such as *Batman Forever*, *Pagemaster*, *Greedy*, and *Renaissance Man*. He is also one of the most environmentally active celebrities in the world. Begley gained an appreciation for the outdoors and natural resources at an early age through Boy Scouts. But it was growing up in the smog of Los Angeles in the 1950s and 1960s that actually motivated him to do something about reducing air and water pollution. He started recycling, using biodegradable soaps and detergents, and doing everything else he could. By 1970, he had become one of the first people in the United States to drive an electric vehicle (EV) as a way to reduce air pollution.

"It was like a golf cart with a windshield wiper," Begley says. "Then I graduated up the transportation ladder to a bicycle, which went farther, faster. Now, I'm driving a new EV-1 made by General Motors. It's one of about 200 of these modern electric vehicles on the road now. In fact, it's the only vehicle I own. I haven't been to a gasoline pump in…years."

Begley sees air and water pollution as two of the biggest threats to our planet today. Because people breathe in air many times per minute, air pollution enters the body very quickly. Water pollution is also a big

Ed Begley, Jr., is one of the most environmentally active celebrities in the world.

concern, since people require clean water to live. With the world's population growing by millions every year, the problems are multiplying.

"Of course, there are other possible threats that we don't understand fully. For instance, we don't know what the ramifications will be from ozone depletion, global warming, and toxic buildup," he says. "It doesn't bode well when you severely alter a system that has a lot to do with the life-support of a planet, and this type of disruption has the potential to really affect life as we know it. There is much more CO_2 [carbon dioxide] in the atmosphere than there was before the Industrial Revolution—everyone agrees on that. What [effects] that extra CO_2 [will have on] the atmosphere and the planet is where there is still some uncertainty and debate. But we do have some warning signs, such as the decline of coral reefs, the decline of amphibians on every continent. These warning signs and others can be compared to a canary in a coal mine—it's not a good sign if the canary is dead."

Begley works in many ways to minimize his and society's impact on the environment. His modest home relies almost exclusively on solar energy. As a result, his annual utility bill is only about $100.

In addition, Begley donates his time to several environmental organizations around the country, including the American Oceans Campaign, Clean Air Coalition, the Environmental Media Association, the Earth Communications Office, the Walden Woods Project, the Environmental Research Foundation, and Greenpeace. He also contributes to individual and local struggles around the country. He says, "I get so many calls from different organizations and individuals that I just try to help put out fires where I can. I try to go wherever the biggest blaze is starting. If I get a call about forestry issues, I will go to Washington, D.C., to attend a conference, or I will go to the Pacific Northwest to attend a rally there. Or [if] people [are] facing a hazardous waste incinerator in Pennsylvania or Michigan, I'll travel there to help them. I also helped a woman and her neighborhood in Houston, who faced an abandoned toxic pit—it was an extreme health threat in the neighborhood. I just go where I'm needed assuming I have the time. If I can't physically get there, I try to be very encouraging over the phone."

Ed Begley, Jr., supports Greenpeace at a 1990 rally regarding hazardous waste.

Begley feels that celebrity involvement with environmental issues is making a difference. Since these famous people have the eyes of the world on them, they have great opportunities to increase awareness, understanding, and support of environmental issues.

"With this opportunity comes tremendous responsibility, though. Celebrities must be knowledgeable about the issues or they lose credibility for themselves and the issues," he explains. "I think people like Dennis Weaver are extremely credible. He lives in a house made of recycled tires and other materials, so he knows what he's talking about. Plus, he supports alternative fuels and is involved in many other issues." Begley also praised Don Henley and Ted Danson for their efforts.

Begley feels that Americans in particular could benefit by following his lead. "It's unfair when 5 percent of the world's population [America] consumes 25 percent of the world's oil. We need to live simply so others can simply live," he remarks, citing a popular expression. "Students should learn more about environmental issues because as populations continue to grow, the stress on natural systems will also continue and we have to live within the caring capacity of that system. The environment is composed of social justice issues and health issues that ultimately affect us all."

The environmental accomplishment of which Begley is most proud has been his ability to live comfortably with less, as a way to reduce his personal environmental impact. Proving that you don't need to go to a gas pump to get around a city like Los Angeles and that you can support a 1990s lifestyle while using solar energy sends a message to others that they can do the same.

A celebrity is usually an actor, actress, musician, or professional athlete, but some businesspeople and politicians draw so much attention that they also become celebrities. Fortunately, some of these people are using their high profiles to help draw attention to environmental problems and solutions.

The decisions that politicians and businesspeople make affect you directly. By being aware of the causes people are involved with, you can support businesses and politicians who are working to protect the environment.

And in combined efforts to benefit the environment, various organizations are enlisting groups of celebrities to help them with their ongoing work. These efforts seek out the assistance of celebrities for activities such as performing on radio shows, donating songs to benefit albums, or helping in the creation of public service announcements. By helping these organizations, committed celebrities are allowing their messages to be heard and understood by much wider audiences.

BUSINESSPEOPLE, POLITICIANS, AND GROUP EFFORTS

Vice-President Al Gore

In a 1994 speech at George Washington University, U.S. Vice-President Al Gore commented that he sees himself and other environmental crusaders as the "Paul Revere[s] of the environment." He hopes to help trigger a revolution before it's too late. "The protection and preservation of the Earth's environment is one of the most important issues facing this generation," Gore says.

After the Democrats won the 1992 election, Gore and U.S. President Bill Clinton announced the Global Climate Change Action Plan, a public-private partnership to reduce greenhouse gas emissions in the atmosphere that affect global warming. The plan aims to develop and distribute more efficient energy and minimize energy demands around the globe. (Global warming is when the average temperature of Earth's atmosphere increases slightly over time. It is caused by the buildup of gases in the upper atmosphere that allows the warmth of the Sun in but traps the heat in the upper atmosphere, much like a greenhouse.)

"The plan is an aggressive attempt to address the world's most important environmental threat. It has 50 separate programs and addresses every source of greenhouse gas emission, in every sector of the economy," Gore says. "It will improve energy efficiency, save businesses, taxpayers, and consumers money, and it will create jobs. Most importantly, it relies on partnerships with states, business, the environmental community and with Congress."

Gore enlisted the support of the scientific community to help justify policy changes to minimize global warming. He also has the support of some people in the business and economic community.

"Guess who made the following statement?" Gore asks. " 'Even a modest 0.9-degree Fahrenheit increase in average global temperature by the year 2010 could

Al Gore has become known as the "environmental vice-president."

produce a 20-day extension of the hurricane season, a 33 percent jump in hurricane landfalls in the United States, an increase in the severity of the storms, and a 30 percent annual rise in U.S. catastrophic losses from storms.' This [is] from a study by the insurance [company], the Travelers Corporation," he answered.

Of course, Gore's environmental concerns include many issues beyond global warming. He also demonstrates how the quality of our air, water, and soil is at risk in his book, *Earth in the Balance: Ecology and the Human Spirit*. He offers his opinion on ozone depletion, rainforest destruction, population trends, and other issues. Gore feels that most of the blame for these problems falls on political leaders who ignore the consequences of timid policy choices. For his continued efforts, Gore will always be known as a vice-president who fought for the environment.

★ *Ted Turner* ★

Ted Turner is one of the most successful businesspeople in America. He is the owner of the Atlanta Braves baseball team and the Atlanta Hawks basketball team, founder of Turner Broadcasting, Inc. (including CNN, Headline News, TBS Superstation, and TNT), and vice chairman of Time Warner Communications. Through his programming, Turner reaches millions of people around the world. He has also become one of the country's most influential environmentalists.

At the foundation of Turner's programming, one can find many shows dedicated to environmental issues. Directed specifically at children is the animated action adventure series, "The New Adventures of Captain Planet." The show tackles environmental offenders through the lives of five youth "Planeteers" who work to stop these problems. When the young heroes join together, they can summon Captain Planet, who is an environmental super hero. Together, Captain Planet and the Planeteers battle eco-villains to stop problems such as drift nets that are trapping not only edible fish, but dolphins, whales, and sea turtles; or pollution that is causing acid rain. Each episode ends with a tip on how to be part of the solution to the Earth's problems.

Ted Turner poses with his environmental super hero Captain Planet.

The award-winning show features the voices of numerous celebrities, including Edward Asner, Whoopi Goldberg, Jeff Goldblum, Levar Burton, and Elizabeth Taylor.

Turner has offered his production resources to produce other environmental programs for adults and children. In addition, he started the Captain Planet Foundation in 1991 to help promote environmental activities for young people. The mission of the foundation is to facilitate and support hands-on environmental projects for children. The objective is to encourage innovative programs that empower children around the world to work both individually and collectively to solve environmental problems in their neighborhoods and communities. Through environmental awareness and education, Turner wants to encourage children to understand and appreciate the world they live in.

Generally, the foundation awards grants for environmental projects for between $250 and $2,500. Funds for the Captain Planet Foundation come from a percentage of the profits generated by the Captain Planet character, as well as corporate contributions.

Some projects that the foundation has funded include environmental field trips, coral reef restoration, wildlife habitat restoration, worm gardens for a classroom, stream monitoring and water-quality programs, organic gardens, and butterfly gardens. Through their website (http://www.turner.com/planet), the foundation also provides links to environmental organizations involved with students.

Despite Turner's busy schedule, he also works to make a difference in other areas. For instance, he has purchased more than 1 million acres of ranch land in Colorado, Montana, New Mexico, and Nebraska, and has begun to restore the native ecosystems on these former cattle ranches. He started by replacing the cattle with bison—once the major inhabitant of the Great Plains ecosystem.

In 1995, Turner hired wildlife biologists to help reestablish the endangered black-tailed prairie dog on his Armendaris Ranch. Shortly thereafter, Turner invited the New Mexico Game and Fish Department to reintroduce the threatened desert bighorn sheep on the ranch's own mountain range—the rugged Fra Cristobals. More than three dozen of the bighorns now roam this new preserve. In the future, Turner also hopes to help reintroduce Mexican wolves and California condors to his Ladder Ranch.

As a result of his efforts to restore biological diversity on the ranches, other species have come back on their own. For instance, at least three pairs of burrowing owls have found the prairie dog colonies and have used some of the tunnels as new nesting sites.

"If rattle snakes were endangered, we would reintroduce them, too," Turner says. "What I'm trying to do with my ranches is to restore the natural ecosystem that evolved over millions of years. If I remember correctly, when Noah built the ark, he didn't turn any animals away."

Ben Cohen and Jerry Greenfield

When Ben Cohen and Jerry Greenfield opened their first ice cream store in an abandoned gas station in 1978, they could not have imagined that their venture would become a famous model for conducting business in a socially responsible manner. Running a business along these lines means tending to the well-being of the community, the environment, and the employees in every aspect of the operation.

In the spring of 1978, in Burlington, Vermont, the pair of fledgling entrepreneurs climbed on top of the old station to patch the roof, place a rock salt and ice freezer in the window, and begin to make what has become a world famous line of premium ice creams and frozen yogurts. Called Ben & Jerry's Homemade, the company now distributes its products in 50 states and has more than 100 franchise locations in 20 states. Many of its ice creams feature innovative flavors such as Rainforest Crunch, sales of which benefit rainforest and environmental preservation, and Phish Food, which benefits Lake Champlain.

Born in 1951 in Brooklyn, New York, just four days apart, Greenfield and Cohen first met in junior high school in the town of Merrick, Long Island. They went their separate ways after high school, but the two met up again in 1977 and decided to go into the food business. They

Ben & Jerry's set up this recycling station at their annual One World One Heart festival in Vermont.

settled on making ice cream and researched the industry before opening their Vermont business.

In 1980, Ben & Jerry's began packing their ice cream in pint containers to distribute them to grocery and convenience stores along their restaurant delivery routes. A year later, in a cover story on ice cream, *Time* magazine called Ben & Jerry's "the best ice cream in the world."

Ben & Jerry's impressive socially responsible mission starts with its commitment to give away 7.5 percent of its pre-tax earnings to benefit society in a number of ways. The company gives money to worthy causes through its foundation, employee-operated Community Action Teams, and other corporate grants.

This commitment has led to many awards, such as being honored at the White House in 1988 as the U.S. Small Business Persons for the year. In addition, President Bill Clinton was quoted in a 1993 issue of *U.S. News & World Report* saying, "It's my favorite ice-cream company because they *do* good and make good ice cream."

"We are all interconnected, and as we help others, we cannot help but to help ourselves in return," Cohen says. "This is a shift from a win-lose situation where it's business versus the environment—to where it's business working with the consumer to improve the quality of life, and business working to improve the quality of the environment at the same time that it makes a profit."

Ben & Jerry's environmental efforts also include activities such as purchasing office supplies made from recycled materials and allowing employees—through their Community Action Teams—to tackle projects such as building nature trails in local parks. In addition, waste ice cream is composted in a Burlington composting effort, where it eventually becomes fertilizer for community gardens. Other ice-cream waste products are used as animal feed, or are spread on farmers' fields directly as fertilizer.

In 1987, the company began feeding pigs at a farm in Stowe, Vermont, with its ice-cream waste. The pigs enjoyed all the flavors except the mint varieties. (It seems they don't like mint.)

"We have always believed—even in the early days of Ben & Jerry's—that our success is to be measured both by our financial gains and by the social impact we achieve by including a concern for the community in our day-to-day business decisions," Ben and Jerry stated in the company's 1993 annual report. "We have made a commitment to be a leader among those who believe that business must assume a greater share of responsibility for the health of our society."

"We are as convinced that our commitment to redefining the social responsibilities of business has been one of the keys to our success," they stated in the following year's report. "As we have supported communities, communities have supported us. We are [as] committed to this vision as we have ever been."

Greenpeace

For more than a decade, the environmental group Greenpeace has relied on numerous rock-and-roll musicians to get its messages heard through face-to-face concert education and fund-raising programs. In 1986, Greenpeace staff members began traveling with various tours to help educate concert goers about environmental issues.

Singer Natalie Merchant performs for Greenpeace at an Earth Day concert.

"Crews of Greenpeace staff help conduct awareness campaigns that reach people all across the country," says Kathy Kane, the organization's music industry liaison. "Our tour project program...educates thousands of...fans about pressing environmental issues affecting us all."

Greenpeace worked with the Grateful Dead to kick off the program in 1986. The Eurythmics, R.E.M., and Tom Petty joined the effort a few years later. In the

The Irish rock band U2 protests with Greenpeace at a nuclear processing plant in 1992.

1990s, musical groups such as Cracker, Gin Blossoms, Smashing
Pumpkins, Red Hot Chili Peppers, Radiohead, Living Colour,
Phish, Guns 'N Roses, Live, Spin Doctors, U2, and Sonic Youth
have also helped the Greenpeace cause.

In working with Tom Petty in 1995, Greenpeace was the only
nonprofit organization with an awareness booth at every show,
enabling the group to reach thousands of concert goers and enroll
more than 300 new members. At one show in New York, the Tom
Petty band refused to go on stage until officials let Greenpeace
set up its information booth inside the arena. The band Phish
also supported Greenpeace and the environment during its 1995
tour. After every show, volunteers calling themselves the "G-Crew"

collected and recycled bottles and cans from concert parking lots. Phish collected nearly one ton of recyclables at larger shows.

Other musicians that have taken part in special projects include Canadian rocker Bryan Adams. His group participated in a postcard campaign. "There is an urgent campaign under way to establish a whale sanctuary in the Antarctic. If it succeeds, it will save most of the whales of the world," Adams wrote on the postcard that was distributed at his concerts. "The danger is, the sanctuary can be blocked by just a handful of countries. Please sign your name and send the postcard....If we all pull together, we can save what's left of the world's whales."

At a 1996 conference, actor Pierce Brosnan supports the Greenpeace stance against nuclear arms.

★ Earth Communications Office ★

After attending an environmental conference in Washington, D.C., in 1988, Bonnie Reiss realized that she could not return to her comfortable life as a lawyer in the entertainment industry. A statement made by a scientist at the event—that the Earth was in a 10- to 20-year window to solve its environmental problems—shocked her into action and changed the course of her life.

Reiss had an idea to use communications to organize various creative leaders in order to serve the global environmental movement. She founded the Earth Communications Office (ECO). By utilizing film, music, and advertising mediums, ECO has since created powerful, award-winning messages about the need to protect the environment. Its empowering messages now reach more than 500 million people annually around the world, inspiring untold actions on behalf of the environment.

ECO's board of directors is composed of leaders from various entertainment and

The ECO enlists the help of many celebrities to produce award-winning environmental messages.

EARTH
COMMUNICATIONS
O F F I C E

communication industries, including famous actors such as Woody Harrelson, Michael Keaton, Pierce Brosnan, Ron Howard, and Ed Begley, Jr. This board works directly with an advisory board made up of environmental, educational, and political leaders to determine the focus of ECO efforts.

One of the nonprofit organization's first big successes involved a short message shown at more than 2,000 movie theaters as a prelude to feature films. The two-minute public service announcement praised the environmental efforts of Americans, stating, "Last year, by recycling paper, you saved 600 million trees. And 22 percent of you carpooled, keeping millions of tons of pollutants out of the air. You recycled 50 percent of all the aluminum cans produced, saving energy and land. And by buying dolphin-safe tuna, you saved 50,000 dolphins. You're making a world of difference." Willie Nelson provided music for the piece by singing, "What a Wonderful World."

In a quiet theater on a big screen, the message created was a powerful, positive reinforcement and was a triumph. Subsequent public service announcements have been seen worldwide. "If people are moved by information that teaches their minds and stirs their hearts, then it can affect everything they do," says Lisa Day, ECO's project director. "If we can move them with information about what is really going on around the globe—and inspire them to believe that they can make a difference—then they'll be creative in ways we can't even imagine."

In 1994, ECO's "Mother" message reminded viewers that Mother Earth has the ability to be humankind's caretaker, provided we take care of her in return. The latest production, "Neighbors," features magnificent footage of ocean life and focuses on the health of the oceans, reminding viewers that

Earth is a water planet and that water sustains all life. This announcement has also been turned into a 30-second television spot, narrated by actor and board member Pierce Brosnan.

ECO consults with, and educates, studios and other communication-based businesses on how to operate their facilities in more environmentally friendly ways. For example, ECO has helped eliminate the use of the rainforest wood Lauan for television- and movie-set construction. The organization also has hosted four conferences over the years to help the entertainment industry understand the many ways it can use the power of communication to promote environmental awareness in the public. In addition, ECO branched out into radio in 1996 with a series of thought-provoking environmental messages.

"The more information and awareness we have about the state of our environment, the better," Day says. "And even more importantly, we need to spread the word about what we all can do to play a positive role in helping ensure that our children inherit a healthy Earth. Judging from the feedback we keep receiving, we feel we've made an impact and hope to continue doing so in the future."

★ ★

The celebrities that you have read about in this book have all made enormous contributions to a great variety of causes. Each one has dedicated his or her time with the hope of making a significant difference in the effort to save our planet. They have fought to protect the rainforest, keep our oceans clean, decrease pesticides in our food, and reintroduce endangered species. They are all exceptional role models who believe that anyone can effect change if they believe in something strongly enough. We thank them for their admirable efforts.

Glossary

activist An especially active and vigorous advocate of a cause.

biodegradable Something that decomposes naturally.

biodiversity The combined diversity of plant and animal species on Earth.

Bureau of Land Management An agency of the federal government that manages public lands and resources.

civil disobedience The refusal to obey certain laws or government demands for the purpose of influencing government legislation or policy. It can entail the use of nonviolent techniques such as boycotting, picketing, or other types of demonstrations.

clear-cut logging Cutting down all of the trees in a section of forest.

commercial development The development of open land with industry, business, or housing.

deforestation Stripping the land of forests.

dilemma Any difficult or perplexing situation or problem.

estuary The portion of the mouth of a river in which the river's current meets the sea's tide, or an inlet of the sea at the lower end of a river.

fungicide A chemical agent that destroys fungi or inhibits their growth.

global warming When carbon dioxide accumulates in the Earth's atmosphere and acts like a layer of insulation, preventing the Earth's heat from escaping to higher elevations where it can cool and return back down in a continual air-and-temperature exchange.

grass-roots movement A movement, usually local, that begins among ordinary people as opposed to movements connected with political parties or other large organizations.

greenhouse gases Gases such as carbon dioxide and ozone that rise to the upper atmosphere and trap the Earth's heat below.

herbicide A chemical agent used to destroy or inhibit plant growth.

hydroelectricity Electricity produced through the dynamic forces of water.

indigenous Having origins in a certain area.

lobby An attempt by an individual or group to get public officials to vote or respond in a particular way.

nonprofit organization An organization that exists to provide a social or other purpose and that does not strive to generate profit for owners.

organic When something is produced naturally without chemical additives; to produce fruits and vegetables without chemical fertilizers or pesticides, and to produce livestock without hormones or antibiotics.

pesticide An agent used to destroy pests.

slash-and-burn farming A practice in which farmers cut down and burn several acres of forest every few years to grow crops. The farmers must keep moving on because the soil only yields a few seasons of crops before it is depleted of minerals. After the farmers move on, the soil usually begins eroding because it won't sustain plant life any more.

source reduction The elimination of pollution and garbage at the source instead of cleaning it up after being released into the environment.

sustainable A practice that can be done in an unlimited manner because of the minimal impact it has on natural resources.

waste management The organization of plans and systems to deal with garbage generation, collection, recycling, reusing, and disposal.

Further Reading

Chandler, Gary and Kevin Graham. *Guardians of Wildlife.* New York: Twenty-First Century Books, 1996.

Cohen, Ben and Jerry Greenfield. *Double Dip: Lead with Your Values and Make Money, Too.* New York: Simon & Schuster, 1997.

Gore, Albert. *Earth in the Balance: Ecology and the Human Spirit.* New York: Houghton Mifflin, 1992.

Henley, Don and Dave Marsh (editor). *Heaven Is Under Our Feet.* Stamford, CT: Longmeadow Press, 1991.

Landau, Elaine. *Environmental Groups.* Hillside, NJ: Lucas, Eileen. *Naturalists, Conservationists, and Environmentalists.* New York: Facts On File, 1994.

Stone, Tanya Lee. *Celebrity Activists: Medical Causes.* New York: Twenty-First Century Books, 1997.

Zeff, Robin. *Environmental Action Groups.* New York: Chelsea, 1993.

For More Information

The Walden Woods Project, 18 Tremont Street, Suite 522, Boston, MA 02108, (800) 554-3569, or e-mail at Waldenwds@aol.com

Honor the Earth, P.O. Box 75423, St. Paul, MN 55101, (800) 327-8407, or the Indigenous Environmental Network, P.O. Box 485, Bemidji, MN 56601, (218) 751-4967

The Rainforest Foundation, 270 Lafayette St., Suite 1205, New York, NY 10012

American Oceans Campaign, (310) 576-6162, or on the Internet at http://www.americanoceans.org

The Captain Planet Foundation, One CNN Center, Atlanta, GA 30303, or on the Internet at http://www.turner.com/planet

Earth Communications Office, 12021 Wilshire Blvd., Box 557, Los Angeles, CA 90025, (310) 571-3141

Index

Photo Credits